SUPERHERO THERAPY
A HERO'S JOURNEY THROUGH ACCEPTANCE AND COMMITMENT THERAPY

Dr Janina Scarlet

Illustrated by Wellinton Alves

ROBINSON

To Andrew McAleer, who changed my life with a single email, to Jay and Matt for believing in me, to my family, by blood or by choice, for their support, and to Dustin McGinnis for being my Superhero.

First published in Great Britain in 2016 by Robinson

1 3 5 7 9 10 8 6 4 2

Important Note
This book is not intended as a substitute for medical advice or treatment. Any person with a condition requiring medical attention should consult a qualified medical practitioner or suitable therapist.

A CIP catalogue record for this book is available from the British Library.

ISBN 978-1-47213-641-1 (paperback)

Designed by Design23, London
Printed in China

Robinson is an imprint of
Little, Brown Book Group
Carmelite House
50 Victoria Embankment
London EC4Y 0DZ

An Hachette UK Company
www.hachette.co.uk

www.littlebrown.co.uk

'Wonderfully written and beautifully illustrated, this engaging book presents Acceptance and Commitment Therapy (ACT) methods using comic book characters from geek culture. It's more than a style – it's a powerful new *method* for using evidence-based therapies to deal with mental health problems. Defusion methods are even more obviously useful when they are 'charms'; it is even clearer what needs to be done when the sword of willingness cuts anxiety monsters down to size. Welcome new recruits to the Superhero Training Academy. I hope you enjoy the super powers you will acquire!'
Steven C. Hayes, Foundation Professor, University of Nevada, Co-developer of ACT

'Dr Janina Scarlet's approach to healing and empowerment is absolutely genius. With her signature blend of compassion, emotional intelligence, honesty and fun, Dr Scarlet's long-awaited Superhero Therapy gives us fascinating insight about the deepest significance of pop culture icons — and an essential guide to creating your own superhero within.'
Chase Masterson, Actress, *Star Trek: Deep Space Nine* and *The Flash*

'Dr Janina Scarlet is a real-life superhero with an origin story to rival any comic book character. After surviving a childhood radiation spill, she moved halfway around the earth, overcame PTSD and chronic pain, and re-invented herself as one of the world's most creative and innovative clinical psychologists. Her Superhero Therapy method is incredibly effective, easy-to-learn, grounded in solid scientific research and, most of all, fun. This book proves that getting stronger and happier can be a creative, intriguing and thrilling journey. I am a huge fan! It has worked for so many people – and I am confident it can work for you.'
Jane McGonigal, PhD, Author of *SuperBetter* and *Reality is Broken*

DID YOU EVER WANT TO BE A SUPERHERO?

CHAPTER 1
A HERO'S JOURNEY BEGINS WITH A STRUGGLE

Have you ever wanted to become a Superhero? Have you ever wished that you could have amazing superpowers, such as super-strength, the ability to fly, or the ability to heal people? Or perhaps you wished that you could travel through time and space, enjoying the many adventures that you would encounter along the way?

Most people I meet wish that they could have special superpowers or magical abilities and most say that if they possessed them, they would use them to help others. One thing I have observed from the years I have spent working with patients with anxiety, depression, post-traumatic stress disorder (PTSD), chronic pain disorder and many other physical and mental health struggles is that most people are capable of a lot more than they know. I have learned that at a time of need, people come to experience superpowers they never knew they had, finding courage, strength and motivation they never believed to be possible.

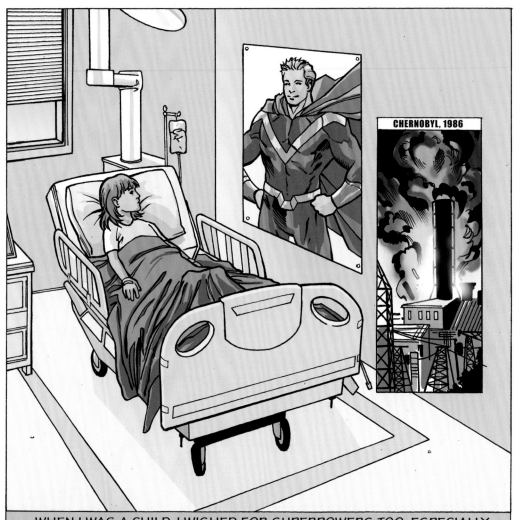

WHEN I WAS A CHILD, I WISHED FOR SUPERPOWERS TOO, ESPECIALLY AT TIMES WHEN I MYSELF FELT 'POWERLESS' AND 'WEAK' AFTER BEING AFFECTED BY THE CHERNOBYL RADIATION SPILL

The truth is that I too for many years wished that I could have magical abilities, specifically, the ability to heal or save people. A traumatic experience I underwent in my early childhood left me feeling 'weak,' 'broken,' and not in control of my own destiny. When I was just a few months shy of my third birthday there was a large nuclear explosion in a city called Chernobyl, not too far away from where my family and I were living in Ukraine. Unfortunately, many of us did not know about the extent of this disaster for nearly a week after the explosion occurred, so we continued eating the fruit and drinking the water, all of which were poisoned.

The radiation spill was catastrophic and left many people, including myself, to experience life-long consequences. For me, the effect was that my immune system shut down, most of my symptoms caused by weather changes. When it was hot outside, I was likely to get an extended nosebleed, landing me in the hospital. When the weather would get chilly, I would be home for weeks with bronchitis. When the barometric pressure would drop before rainfall, I was sure to get a migraine, or worse, a seizure.

THE RADIATION SPILL CAUSED MY IMMUNE SYSTEM TO MALFUNCTION, LEADING TO TREMENDOUS AMOUNTS OF PAIN AND CHRONIC ILLNESS WHICH WOULD GET WORSE WHEN IT WOULD RAIN

As I lay in my hospital bed after yet another seizure, feeling weak and powerless, I dreamt of having strength. I dreamt of being healthy. I dreamt of being able to cure and inspire people who were going through a difficult time, the very ones who often thought about giving up. Like I did.

I was twelve when my family and I moved to the United States. I thought that things would get better if I was away from radiation. I was both right and wrong. While my health improved after our move, my overall situation did not. Most of my classmates at school did not understand what radiation was, nor did they know what seizures were. Like so many of the people reading this book, I was heavily bullied. It wasn't uncommon for me to overhear my classmates telling each other that I was 'radioactive'. Many people would refuse to use things I had touched, like pencils, mistakenly believing me to be contagious.

I felt alone. I felt like no one would understand how depressed I was and how much I hated myself.

On most days I just wanted to die.

It all changed when I saw the first movie about the 'Super Mutants'. At the time I did not know who the Super Mutants were and while I read a lot of fantasy books, I had not yet got into comics. The movie became my portal into the world of superheroes, where people with super-abilities used these powers to help others. Most importantly, this was the first time I was able to find characters I connected with. The characters were mutants, all with some kind of genetic modification, just like me. My favourite of all of them was Thunder because she could control the weather, a power I wished I could also have since my own maladies were all weather-related.

It was after seeing this film that I first became fascinated with the idea of using fictional characters, like superheroes, to help myself and others overcome difficult emotional experiences. As I began analysing my favourite fictional characters I noticed something – most of them underwent an excruciating personal experience, which shaped their personality and made them the very hero that they eventually became. Think about it: most of the fictional characters you know probably experienced some kind of a deep personal struggle, such as losing their parents, somehow being different and feeling alienated from other people, or being forced into a heroic journey that they felt unprepared to be a part of. Some faced loss along the journey, underwent deep traumatic experiences, had doubts and battled depression or addiction. Sound familiar?

IT OCCURRED TO ME THAT MOST HEROES GO THROUGH SOME KIND OF A STRUGGLE OR A PAINFUL EXPERIENCE AND IT IS THE CHOICES THEY MAKE, RATHER THAN THEIR SPECIAL ABILITIES, THAT MAKE THEM SUPERHEROES
Neil Scott
Shadow Gray
Monica Mercury
Doctor Apeiron Semper
Katrina Quest
Drovin

Many people (myself included), when facing these struggles, might view them as a sign of personal weakness and might be too discouraged to continue their heroic mission. But what if these struggles are not a sign of weakness? What if the very struggle you are going through is a representation of deep interpersonal strength that only you could experience? What if the very thoughts, feelings and physical sensations that you have struggled with were merely obstacles to be overcome on your own superhero journey? And what if there was a way to help guide you on your superhero path?

Every hero has a mentor or a sidekick to help them along their journey and I can be yours. Together we can learn how to battle the black dogs of depression, slay the anxiety dragons, release the binding ropes of trauma and avoid the snakes of addiction temptation. Superhero therapy uses methods from evidence-based (research-supported) therapies, such as acceptance and commitment therapy (ACT), as well as other research-supported interventions, such as self-compassion. All are known to help people better manage their anxiety, depression, PTSD and addiction (including overeating), as well as to improve healthy behaviours such as exercising, socializing with others and gaining courage; in essence becoming the kind of hero that they always wanted to be.

In order for us to be able to track your progress, please take a few minutes to answer the following questions with a True or False response. You will also take the same survey when you are finished with your superhero training in order to measure your progress.

1. My symptoms overwhelm me   T/F
2. I must get rid of my depression/anxiety/shame/anger   T/F
3. I spend most of my time worrying about the future   T/F
4. I spend a lot of my time fixating on the past   T/F
5. My self-critical thoughts (such as 'I'm not good enough' or
   'I'm not attractive enough') have become my identity   T/F
6. I don't spend enough time doing things I care about   T/F
7. I am unhappy with many aspects of my life   T/F

How many 'T's and how many 'F's do you have? Write down the exact number. Notice any judgements or painful emotions that may arise when you are answering these questions. Remember that just like you, most people struggle with very similar difficulties. You are not alone in this.

We are going to take this journey together. I recommend that you read one chapter each week, either by yourself, with a friend, or with your therapist. Each chapter introduces a new superhero skill and gives you a chance to practise it. Some skills might be easier for you than others, and some skills you might find more useful than others. Feel free to modify your own superhero training programme in any way that best supports your current needs. Many people find it helpful to get a notebook, perhaps one with a picture of your favourite real-life or fictional hero on it, in order to inspire you and help you keep track of your progress.

The book will demonstrate training for six different heroes – Shadow Gray, Katrina Quest, Doctor Apeiron Semper, Drovin, Neil Scott and Monica Mercury. Although these characters are fictional, their struggles are real, as they are based on some of my patients in real life.

In short, welcome to your Superhero Training Academy. I am extremely grateful to have you along for the journey. Are you ready to begin?

MANY OF US WISH TO BECOME A
SUPERHERO, INHERIT MAGICAL POWERS
OR GET THE CHANCE TO ESCAPE OUR
CURRENT PREDICAMENT

BUT WHAT IF IT HAPPENED?
WHAT IF YOU ACTUALLY WERE
ABLE TO BECOME THE VERY
HERO YOU IMAGINED?

WHAT IF THE PAIN DIDN'T HURT ANY MORE
AND YOU WERE NO LONGER AFRAID?

HOW WOULD YOUR LIFE
LOOK THEN?

MONSTERS (FROM LEFT TO RIGHT):
ANXIETY, SHAME, ANGER AND DEPRESSION

CHAPTER 2
AVOIDING THE MONSTERS MAKES THEM STRONGER

Monica Mercury holds a razor to her arm. Her depression monster whispers gently in her ear. 'Just end it. Things will never get any better and you know it.'

Will this be the day that she ends it all? The thought has crossed Monica's mind and after careful consideration she makes a precise incision. The trickling blood seems almost soothing, temporarily taking away the feelings of overwhelming depression and self-disgust. The self-disgust is always particularly active every time she looks in the mirror.

When she looks at her reflection again, the shame monster is especially ruthless. 'Ugh, you're disgusting! It's no wonder everyone hates you. You're fat and ugly and no one will ever love you!'

A few more strokes of the razor and the monster seems satisfied. Just to be fully sure that he doesn't come back that day, Monica sticks her fingers in the back of her throat in a familiar fashion.

Between the vomiting and the cutting rituals she feels more in control, far less of a victim to her classmates' bullying and her own mind's torments. And yet, even in these moments she is still struggling; feeling in control and at the same time feeling excruciatingly alone.

As Monica forces herself to vomit, the anxiety monster has officially begun its shift. 'What if someone at school found out you were bulimic? They'd torture you even more than they already do. What if they lock you up in some hospital? What if you vomit in class tomorrow? What if the gym teacher sees the scars on your arms?'

Monica feels her chest tighten, her jaw squeezing shut, and her fists clenching. Feeling as if someone punched her in the stomach. Feeling alone. Empty.

Like Monica, many of us have these monsters of shame and anxiety, and although we might go through different kinds of agonizing rituals in order to appease them, we might still struggle with the overwhelming effects they have on us. This effort of trying to reduce any kind of emotionally painful experience is called *experiential avoidance*. Monica's vomiting in order to appease her monsters is an example of experiential avoidance, where Monica is attempting to reduce and avoid her painful thoughts and feelings.

How does experiential avoidance work? It is like a bribe we might give to a bully. In the short term, it usually makes us feel better: the bullies/monsters are likely to temporarily suspend their abuse. However, in the long term, the bully inevitably comes back and usually demands an even greater sacrifice.

We can also think of experiential avoidance as a trap or a trick set up by an evil villain trying to prevent us from succeeding in our quest. On the surface, it might seem like a good compromise – do what the villain asks and she will leave you alone. This process of giving in to the demands of our internal villains in order to reduce the internal struggle is called *negative reinforcement*. The word 'negative' here refers to something being taken away, in this case, the monster's torture. And the word 'reinforcement' refers to us being more likely to continue this behaviour in the future.

A great example of negative reinforcement is substance abuse. When people are overwhelmed by their personal suffering, they might, for example, drink alcohol in order to feel better. In this case, the alcohol will provide a temporary relief from the monster's abuse. However, the villain is greedy and once the effects of alcohol wear off, the monster will return, stronger and louder, ensuring that the person is likely to continue using alcohol. Think of it as like trying to fight a hydra – the more we might try to behead it, the more heads it will generate.

In many ways this is what Doctor Semper is attempting to do. Semper's job is to travel through time and space in his Hurricane Simulator and save people. He prided himself on being kind and able to rescue others. Recently however, Doctor Semper experienced a tragic loss – he was unable to rescue a little girl, who ended up falling to her death. He still plays out the moments leading up to her death in his mind. He experiences guilt over what happened to her. He used to feel in control of his own fate and secure in his ability to help others.

That is no longer the case.

To make matters worse, last month Semper experienced something he never had before in his 4550 years of living. When he stepped out of the Simulator, his three hearts all started pounding extremely fast in his chest, it was as if he had run around the galaxy four times without stopping (and he hadn't done that in at least 500 years). In addition to the overwhelming heartbeats, the Doctor's breathing became very fast and shallow. Semper began shaking uncontrollably, he was sweating, his vision became extremely blurry, his stomachs felt as if they would turn inside out, and he was sure that this time he was going to die for good.

Doctor Semper called out for his assistant, an Earth-born neuroscientist named Andrea, who helped him back into the Simulator. Strangely, when he was back inside his time machine, the Doctor felt better. His heart rates reduced back to normal, his breathing rate slowed down, he was no longer shaking and over time his vision returned to normal. Andrea explained to him that he had had what is called a *panic attack*, something a lot of Earthlings have, especially after they have an experience of not being in control of a specific situation.

Although Doctor Semper felt significantly better after returning to the Simulator, he found that because he was overwhelmed by his panic attack, he was unable to leave the Simulator without Andrea's assistance. If he stepped more than twenty feet away from the Simulator, he started having similar symptoms – the racing hearts, shallow breathing, shaking, and sweating.

At these times, his anxiety monster shouted at him, 'You're going to die! You can't handle it! It's not safe! You're going to go crazy!'

Not wanting to experience another panic attack, the Doctor ran back into the Simulator. The only times he was able to get more than 20 feet away from his safety zone was when Andrea was with him.

This is in fact what happens to a lot of people who develop *panic disorder* and *agoraphobia*. The fear of additional attacks might prevent the person from going to places or participating in activities where panic attacks might be likely. At the same time, being too far away from a safety object (such as a time machine or someone's home or car) or a safety buddy (such as a companion, a family member or a pet) might also trigger the feelings of anxiety.

And just like Monica, Doctor Semper initially felt better after avoiding his feared outcome – an environment he could not control. However, in the long term, he felt less capable of handling this situation, which only served to strengthen the belief that the outside world is dangerous.

AVOIDANCE OFTEN CREATES THE VERY OUTCOME WE ARE TRYING TO AVOID AND USUALLY INCREASES SHAME

For the majority of people, fictional or otherwise, avoidance of a feared outcome might make them more stressed out and might actually create the very consequence that they are trying to avoid. For example, Neil Scott struggles with social anxiety disorder (SAD), where he fears social humiliation and feels extremely anxious when he has to make a presentation or ask someone out on a date. His anxiety began when he was a small child and was physically and emotionally abused by his parents. As a result, Neil now puts himself down in social situations.

Since he began studying at the Wizarding College six months ago, Neil's social anxiety has only gotten worse. Neil believes that he got into the school by mistake, or that he is somehow a 'fraud' and that soon enough everyone will find out that he is 'not good enough' to be there. Neil was always shy but his 'fraud syndrome' makes him especially self-conscious, causing him to have frequent anxiety and panic attacks when he has to demonstrate his knowledge in front of the class or talk to others.

In order to prove his worthiness, Neil spends hours studying different charms and incantations and does well on his own. However, whenever a professor asks him to demonstrate a spell in front of the classroom, Neil's heart begins to pound loudly in his chest (in fact, he sometimes wonders if others can hear it). He sweats so much that he believes that everyone can see the perspiration covering his vividly blushing face. Even though he knows the required spells, his anxiety monster causes Neil an overwhelming amount of fear of looking foolish in front of the class. As a result, Neil simply states that he does not know the answer in order to be allowed to sit back down at his desk.

The same thing occurs whenever Neil likes someone. Last week, for instance, he saw a wizard he fancies, Brian, sitting across from him at the dining hall. He felt his heart warm when he saw Brian smile at him. Trying to work up the courage to ask him out on a date, Neil attempted to stand up. However, his anxiety monster beat him to it.

'Don't even think about it!' The anxiety monster yelled at him. 'If you ask him out, he'll reject you and laugh at you, and you'll be all alone, as always.'

His shoulders and fists tensed, he felt his stomach turn in knots and he sat back down in defeat. Several minutes later Brian walked past him but Neil did not dare look at him. Neil's shame monster was already doing what he did best – putting him down.

In both of these examples, Neil's experiential avoidance of the anxiety-producing situations created the very outcome that Neil was trying to avoid. In attempts to avoid looking foolish, he refused to answer the professor's question, only presenting himself as less capable than if he had attempted it. In addition, by not asking Brian out on a date, Neil made certain that he ended up alone, feeling ashamed and rejected, the very feelings he was trying to avoid. However, in addition to ensuring the unwanted outcome to occur, experiential avoidance also guarantees an added dose of shame for failing to take the chance in the first place.

Often when fear prevents us from taking a chance on something we really care about, we are likely to experience regret. In fact, at the end of their lives the majority of people do not regret their successes or failures but rather the chances they did not take. By avoiding something that is really important to us, we are more likely to experience shame, harsh self-criticism, and confirm our (often mistaken) beliefs that we are not capable of succeeding at a particular task.

For most people, experiential avoidance makes it more likely that they are going to experience more anxiety, more depression or worse, chronic pain, making them more likely to get or maintain certain mental health disorders. In fact, many mental health disorders are maintained or made worse by avoidance as is the case with obsessive-compulsive disorder (OCD), specific phobia (such as the fear of spiders, snakes, heights, flying and others), substance abuse disorders, eating disorders, post-traumatic stress disorder (PTSD) and others.

Very frequently the attempts to control and avoid difficult emotional experiences are more likely to make us worse rather than better. This means that the real enemies are not the symptoms. The real enemy is avoidance, a trap set up by a villain to ensure that we fail before we even attempt to begin our hero's journey.

Luckily, the avoidance trap can be overcome and in the following chapters we are going to learn the different skills we will need to ensure success battling the avoidance villains and becoming a true superhero. Specifically, we are going to learn how to manage the four common monsters that frequently try to prevent us from living the kind of life that we might fantasize about. These monsters are anxiety, depression, shame and anger. In addition, we are going to learn to utilize our own sidekicks, like hope, resilience, courage and self-compassion.

To ensure your success, at the end of each chapter I will recommend Superhero Steps to practise. These will strengthen your superhero training to better help you on your heroic journey.

SUPERHERO STEPS

Notice when you might avoid something. Notice how you feel in the short and long term. Don't feel obligated to change anything at this point. Just observe and collect data, it will be helpful later.

Are you ready?

Fasten your cape, adjust your utility belt, here we go!

DREADING THE IMAGINED FUTURE

CHAPTER 3
TRAINING YOUR MIND TO BE A HERO'S MIND

As Katrina Quest approaches her new car, she immediately feels her heart rate increase. With her sweaty hands she attempts to put the key in the door to open it but her hands are shaking too much to allow her to do this.

She does not even have time to close her eyes when the flashbacks begin. Suddenly she is back there, at the scene of the accident. A drunken truck driver has crashed into her, nearly killing her. It is as if she is right there again, seeing the truck right in front of her, seeing the windshield shatter.

Even now, nearly a year after that event, she can still see it and almost feel it in her body. Her shoulders tighten so much that she looks completely stiff.

Frozen with fear, her heart pounding, she stands next to her car as her anxiety monster yells out, 'This is not safe! You're going to die!' Katrina stands frozen as she tries to remember how to breathe again. She is forced to relive her past until her body gives in and allows her to cry as a form of relief.

Katrina is a superhero who uses her ability to fly in order to help other people. However, since she was in an accident, Katrina has neither been able to drive nor fly. The car accident caused her to develop a driving phobia, along with a flying phobia. In addition, she struggles with symptoms of post-traumatic stress disorder (PTSD).

After experiencing a traumatic event, such as a car accident, we are likely to replay that scenario over and over again in our minds. We might therefore be living in our past or, as is also the case for Katrina, be scared about our future. Katrina expects that every time she will get behind the wheel, she will get into an accident again. She also believes that the same will happen if she flies, even though she has never been injured while flying. Her constant worries about the possibility of getting into another accident are preventing her from experiencing what is truly happening in the present moment.

On the other hand, Shadow Gray is living in the past. Shadow is a demon hunter. Armed with a crossbow and sarcasm, Shadow and her team typically roam the streets of their hometown, hunting demons and protecting human beings. But sometimes demons are not the scariest beasts that humans need to fear. Two years ago, Lorion, a fellow demon hunter, attacked Shadow and sexually assaulted her. She trusted him. He violated that trust. To this day Shadow feels hurt, 'weak,' and 'broken'.

When she told her friends about the incident, some of them did not believe her, while others told her that she should consider dating Lorion, because he is 'such a great guy.' Two years later, Shadow is still haunted by the memory of what happened to her. Her friends fail to understand why she can't 'just get over it and move on' since the assault happened 'so long ago.' Over the past six months, Shadow has begun distancing herself from her friends and stopped going out on demon patrols, as she did not believe she was capable of helping herself, let alone others. Shadow struggles with PTSD, depression, and shame about what happened to her, as well as guilt for 'not being able to prevent it.'

Katrina's and Shadow's experiences are sadly not uncommon and the painful incidents of our past might affect our beliefs about the future. One of the best elixirs for difficult experiences is mindfulness. Mindfulness refers to purposely observing our experiences in real time and without judging them (as 'bad' for example). More specifically, it refers to noticing our thoughts, feelings, behaviours, our five senses (sight, taste, smell, sound and touch), and the environment around us. You can think of it as like a healing potion in a video or table-top role-playing game. This magic potion might not taste good but it is helpful with recovery, meaning that experiencing anxiety, depression or other painful sensations can be unpleasant but allowing ourselves to feel them may help us to recover in the long term.

WHY MINDFULNESS?

Researchers actually find that when we are anxious, overwhelmed, traumatized, or otherwise distressed, our minds begin to wander. Usually our minds go into problem-solving mode by default and often focus on something negative, like an embarrassing moment or an anxious thought. Scientists find that the more our mind wanders, the unhappier we are likely to be. With that we might also feel more anxious, more stressed, more depressed, and might be more likely to try to avoid these sensations (which, if you remember, is a villain trap), potentially leading to us becoming more likely to be emotionally and physically unhealthy.

MINDFUL – ENGAGING THE SENSES

There is a saying, 'Name it and you tame it,' which suggests that mindfully acknowledging our emotions might make them less overwhelming. Imagine if rather than running away from the monsters, you could see and acknowledge them, as if they were wearing name tags, almost as if to say, 'Hello, my name is Anxiety.' In fact, if we were to notice the emotion of anxiety, we might also notice the physiological changes that it brings, such as rapid heartbeat, shallow breathing and muscle tension, especially in the upper back, neck and shoulders. For some people anxiety also leads to a clenched jaw and jaw pain, tight wrists, sweating and other symptoms. Spending time noticing these symptoms might alert us that we need to roll our shoulders back, unclench our jaw and perhaps focus on our breathing. If we ignore these symptoms, the body is more likely to keep increasing our anxiety symptoms in order to get our attention. On the other hand, mindfully noticing these symptoms, and spending some time experiencing each one, often might reduce these symptoms.

I want to be clear here – mindfulness is not itself an anti-anxiety tool. This means that mindfulness will not make us anxiety-free, although it often feels relaxing and might lead to a reduced anxiety state. However, this is more of a side effect and not an expectation.

Practising mindfulness is kind of like having a wise mentor, like an elderly wizard or a knight trainer. Sometimes the mentor might be encouraging and make you feel better about yourself. Sometimes, however, the mentor might point out a skill that you may be struggling with, which might not necessarily feel good to hear. However, the mentor's words will be helpful to you in better knowing your practice, and it will always be wise.

In essence, mindfulness practice is kind of like having a LifeLink (an enchantment that can extend life) in a game. In fact, scientists are finding that regular mindfulness practice reduces stress and better regulates blood pressure, as well as reducing anxiety, depression, PTSD symptoms chronic pain symptoms, and leading to better outcomes for eating and substance abuse disorders. In addition, mindfulness has also been found to improve romantic relations and potentially prolong life.

NOTICING THE EMOTIONS

MINDFULNESS IN PRACTICE

Now that we know that mindfulness is an essential part of your superhero training, how do we begin to practise it? One quick mindfulness exercise I like to use both for myself and for my patients is the 'Where are my feet?' practice. I sometimes refer to it as 'quick and dirty' or 'mindfulness for busy people' because it does not take very long to complete. In order to do this practice, we need to ask ourselves, 'Where are my feet?' and notice where our feet* are at the present moment. The feet will usually be on the ground, or at times elevated, or perhaps stepping on the car accelerator or brakes. This practice might immediately ground us by reminding us where we are at a given moment and that neither the painful past nor the dreaded future, are happening right now.

A slightly longer mindfulness practice includes focusing on the five senses: sight, sound, smell, taste and touch. There are numerous ways of practising mindfulness that involve engaging the senses. One way could be to allocate a period of time (for example, ten minutes) for sitting still and focusing on one sense at a time. Another way could be to spend a couple of minutes just practising noticing your surroundings, such as the colours, shapes and all kinds of details (large and small) in your environment. Then you can focus on the sounds that you might be able to hear and so on.

* For people with a physical disability that prevents them from making contact with their feet or for people who are missing limbs, the exercise can alternatively focus on a different part of the body, for example, the hands, the jaw or the tongue.

MINDFULNESS IS NON-JUDGEMENTAL PRESENT MOMENT AWARENESS

Another mindfulness exercise involves focusing on the breath. Just as with the five senses exercise, we can set aside approximately ten minutes (or more if possible) to bring awareness to our breath. We can focus on the sensations that come up when we inhale and exhale. There are a number of smartphone apps and guided mindfulness recordings available on the Internet.

If your life is too hectic to be able to spend ten minutes a day on a mindfulness exercise, then you can consider incorporating mindfulness into your everyday routine. For example, when taking a shower you can notice the feel of the water on your body and the sound it makes, while also noticing the scent of the soap and seeing the soap bubbles around you. You might be able to also practise this while brushing your teeth, eating a meal, or drinking tea or coffee. The latter example, about engaging our senses while eating or drinking, is called *savouring*. Very often when we are eating, we might quickly finish our meal without fully enjoying it, sometimes without fully noticing what or how much we have eaten. The savouring practice consists of taking the time to use our senses to fully enjoy the specific experience, such as eating.

Another part of mindful savouring can include a gratitude practice. Gratitude refers to giving mindful appreciation for something or someone. Gratitude does not have to be about something major, it could be about anything, such as a morning cup of coffee, about what someone might have done for us at one point, or about a particular memory. The research on gratitude suggests that a daily gratitude practice of naming one to three things for which we are grateful can reduce anxiety, depression, stress and other benefits.

See if you can name one thing you are grateful for today. It does not have to be big, for example, your friends, family, your abilities or your interests. If you are not in a place where you can do this today, that is OK too. Just notice this difficulty without judgement and notice what's happening in your body as you experience it. In fact, gratitude practice is not always easy and sometimes when we've been through a really hard time, we might struggle to find things to be grateful for. That is perfectly normal and if you are unable to find anything to be grateful for today, that is no problem, we can try again tomorrow. In addition, I would like to point out that it is also possible to feel grateful while feeling what seem to be conflicting emotions, like anger, shame and resentment.

For example, Neil might have a lot of shame about struggling with his magic classes but at the same time he is also grateful for the opportunity to attend the Wizarding College.

As we are starting to get deeper into your superhero training, I am going to ask you to practise mindfulness this week every day in whichever way is available to you – either by noticing where your feet are, focusing on your five senses, mindful savouring (for example, music, food or tea), doing breathing practice, or gratitude practice. If you are struggling with any of these or if they bring pain or discomfort, notice that too and see if you can also notice what your body might need (for example, rest, food or relaxation).

OBSTACLES TO MINDFULNESS

Some of the biggest obstacles to practising mindfulness have to do with mistaken beliefs that some people have about this practice. Very often when I talk to my patients about mindfulness they might say that they have tried it at one point and found that 'it wasn't working': Most people who first attempt to practise mindfulness believe that mindfulness means taking a lotus posture and meditating for hours and hours without having a single thought. That is actually not accurate.

Mindfulness is essentially an awareness training, which tends to be especially helpful with physical and psychological health. It can involve a meditation practice but it does not have to. Furthermore, it is not accurate that mindfulness (or meditation for that matter) means that we are expected to not have any thoughts. In fact, it is not possible to sit for more than a few minutes without a single thought because our minds naturally wander. Even lifelong experienced meditators get distracted while meditating. The goal of a mindfulness practice then is to notice when the attention shifts to something else and to gently bring it back to the present task without judging ourselves for this. If while you are practising being mindful of your breath or your five senses you notice that your thoughts drift to think about the work you still have to do, congratulations! You are doing exactly what you're supposed to. Notice that you got distracted and gently bring your attention back to your current mindfulness task.

Another potential obstacle involves our expectation that a mindfulness practice will always feel good or will always make us feel good. This is not the case. Some times practising mindfulness might be relaxing, while others might be difficult as we might become aware of something that's bothering us, physically or emotionally. This is actually a good thing because we then become aware of what we might need. You can think of this practice as tuning into your time machine or your spaceship. Mindfulness might help you be better equipped to operate your time machine and it might make you aware of any potential technical issues that need to be addressed.

SUPERHERO STEPS

This week I recommend that you try to set aside some time to practise your superhero mindfulness training daily. This might include being mindful of your breathing or five senses, or perhaps a meditation practice if you already have one. Feel free to use phone apps or download guided meditations for this practice, if you would like.

If setting time aside to practise mindfulness is impossible on certain days, then practise mindfulness on the go – ask 'Where are my feet?' and paying attention to your senses while doing other tasks, such as eating, showering or commuting.

CHAPTER 4
YOUR SUPERHERO SELF

Whenever he closes his eyes, Drovin still sees the images from the Space War. He can still smell the cauterizing odour of the laser beams cutting into human flesh. He can see his best friend jOrrin's body, or rather the pieces that remain. He still remembers picking up the cold limp pieces off the ground and packing him up to be shipped back to his family. Drovin also remembers the anger he felt towards the enemy troops. He does not remember opening fire but he does recall his Commander throwing him on the ground after Drovin had killed two unarmed people on the opposing side.

I'm evil, Drovin told himself.

Two weeks prior to him starting at the Superhero Training Academy, Drovin was sitting in his apartment, back on his home planet Kridaq, located on the north-west arm of the Pinwheel Galaxy. In his left hand he held a remote to the Intergalactic television projection device, and in his right he held a bottle of locally made beer, Pobég. Mindlessly changing the channels, he was not actually aware of what he was watching. His mind was back to that moment when he first saw jOrrin's body.

Periodically, he would also flash back to the incident that occurred three months previously, when Drovin was back home with his family. Drovin's four year-old son, Zeelik, accidentally spilled a carton of milk and walked away without cleaning it up. Drovin's patience had been very short since he returned from the war and he could not tolerate his son's apparent lack of responsibility.

Tense and hot with fury, Drovin grabbed Zeelik's arm, almost twisting it, dragged him to the kitchen and shouted, 'When you spill something, you clean it up! Why is that so hard to understand?' Zeelik's cries only make Drovin angrier and it wasn't until his wife intervened that he let go of his son.

I'm evil, he reminded himself again.

When his wife left him and took Zeelik with her, Drovin believed that it was for the best, as he did not believe that they were safe around him.

What Drovin is essentially experiencing is an attachment to an identity he created for himself. By believing that he is evil, Drovin is in some ways acting according to this adapted identity. Most people, when presented with a highly traumatic situation, are going to be affected by it and many might do something that is otherwise out of character for them, like hurting their loved ones. Many trauma survivors I have worked with, including military service members with combat trauma, like Drovin; or sexual assault survivors, like Shadow; or people who witnessed homicide or torture; or former gang members, might develop a new sense of self, such as 'I'm evil,' 'I'm weak' or 'I'm broken.' Most of the time, however, people base these stories on an incident that was out of their control and occurred over a short period of time (on average, one to two minutes).

We all have such self-stories. I have one too. Mine is 'I'm an amateur.' I still remember when it first happened. I believe I was about six to seven years old when I wrote my first short story. I was so excited by it. It was going to be a bestseller! Excited and beaming with pride and joy I showed my 'masterpiece' to my brother. My brother is nine years older than me and was the kind of guy that guys wanted to be friends with and girls wanted to date. In short, my brother was *cool*.

'So, what do you think?' I asked him, awaiting generous praise.

But it never came. My brother turned his hand over and down again, the kind of gesture that people might make when they are neither overly pleased nor overly disappointed with their evening meal.

'Ehhh. It's kind of amateur,' he replied.

Amateur.

That was the first day I learned that word. He was completely right of course, if not overly generous. However, the six-year-old me took this word to heart so much so that I stopped writing for many years. To this day, when I give a talk, whenever I teach, and even now, writing this book, this self-story is triggered – 'I'm an amateur,' which in turn triggers other self-stories, such as 'I'm not good enough,' or 'I'm a fraud and everybody will find out.'

Still waiting for the 'fraud police' to find me, I realized that by over-identifying with this self-story, I was holding myself back and not taking the kind of chances that would be most meaningful to me. In a lot of ways, by not even trying due to my believed *not good-enoughness*, I was essentially setting myself up for failure. If this sounds familiar to you, that is because this is a fairly universal experience.

In fact, over time our self-stories can start to control our behaviour by essentially turning into a *self-fulfilling prophecy*. A self-fulfilling prophecy is (usually) a false prediction, inadvertently made true by the people who believe in it. For Drovin, the story that he tells himself is that he is 'evil' or 'damaged' and as a result he might distance himself from others or become more aggressive toward them. For Doctor Semper, his self-story is 'I'm incapable' and 'I'm not brave enough.'

Self-stories don't always have to include self-judgements. Sometimes they contain specific roles we believe we ought to play, which (frequently) include unspoken rules of how we are expected to act. For example, Shadow is a demon hunter and in over-identifying with this identity, she might believe that a demon hunter must be someone who *never* cries, someone who is *never* 'weak.' She might then either try to hide her own feelings in order to try to fit into the role that she believes is expected of her, or she might believe that she is 'not capable' of being a demon hunter.

The opposite of these over-identified self-stories is what is called *self-as-context*, or as I like to refer to it, *your superhero self*. These are unlike self-stories, which are usually not only unhelpful but oftentimes also limiting. The connection with your superhero self is a reminder that you can practise being you in any environment, in any situation, no matter the circumstances. What it means is that no matter how young or old you are, no matter what happens to you, you can still be your superhero self, whatever that might mean to you.

One exercise I like to practise with all my superheroes is to have them write one self-story item on a sticky note and then put it on themselves. The first one people usually think of has to do with negative judgements, such as 'I'm fat,' 'I'm unlovable,' or 'I'm not good enough.' In fact, none of the single sticky notes represent the big picture, the real you. However, we usually self-story one or two of them, usually the harshest, the most self-critical ones, and over-identify with it, as if it's the absolute truth about us. As the exercise continues, other aspects of one's over-identified self might present themselves. Pretty soon, the person might be fully covered with sticky notes, the real superhero self hidden somewhere underneath them.

For example, Doctor Semper's superhero self consists of many different parts. He is a time-travelling scientist from another planet. He is also someone who values saving people. He is heroic and he is also someone who gets scared sometimes. He is compassionate and kind, he is creative and loyal and he is someone who likes strange foods, such as cheese sticks in chocolate sauce. All of these make up his superhero self. No matter where he is, no matter whom he is with, no matter what happens to him, Doctor Semper can remind himself of who he really is. Being true to ourselves, transcending time and our life circumstances, is one of the most courageous things that we can do.

In fact, it was his sense of his true self, his superhero self, which reminded the Doctor that he is someone who is passionate about helping others. This is what prompted Doctor Semper to arrive on Planet Kridaq that fateful morning in order to try to convince Drovin to come to the Superhero Training Academy with him. Unfortunately for Doctor Semper, Drovin's angry refusal to come with him to the Training Academy, coupled with Semper being more than twenty feet away from the Simulator, sparked the Doctor's beliefs, such as 'I'm incapable,' and caused him to have a panic attack.

Feeling his hearts pounding in his chest, he began to shake, trying to breathe, which suddenly became extremely laborious. Doctor Semper leaned on the wall, scared that he was going to faint. His stomach tightening into knots, his brain feeling like mush, Semper wasn't sure if he was going to die or lose his mind.

He suddenly felt a warm heavy hand on his shoulder. It was Drovin.

'Hey, it's OK, man,' Drovin said softly. There was a genuine sense of concern in his voice. He helped the Doctor back into his ship and, after some negotiating, agreed to come to the Academy with him, though convinced that it was not going to be helpful.

It is not unusual for us to think that a particular situation is hopeless when we are going through a hard time. One of the reasons this happens is that we might begin to think of ourselves in terms of unhelpful self-stories. However, the truth is that no matter what happens to us, we are still that same superhero. As a way to remind ourselves of that, we could practise the superhero-self grounding meditation.

SUPERHERO SELF GROUNDING MEDITATION

Get into a comfortable position, sitting or lying down. See if you can close your eyes and begin to bring your attention to your body. Notice the bottoms of your feet and where your feet are at this moment. Notice if they are warm or cold, tired or relaxed, tense or comfortable.

Perhaps placing your hands on your heart, see if you can recall the first time you ever wanted to be a hero. See if you can remember a time when you helped someone, when you really made a difference. What was that like? Do you notice the sensations in your heart as you recall this?

Throughout your life you have probably experienced many obstacles and changes. Your hair might have changed, your face might have changed, your tastes and preferences might have changed too. However, the one thing that remains is your superhero self; that part of you that wants to make a difference. And through all the changes you ever encounter, the one thing that will remain the same is your superhero self. It is here for you always. It is who you are, the very core of your being no matter what life might throw at you.

Take a few moments to reflect on this experience and once you are finished, open your eyes.

SUPERHERO STEPS

We spend so much time essentially zooming in on the aspects of our personality/appearance that we don't like, but we should also consider the other aspects of our superhero self, including the neutral ones, and the ones we like.

This week practice identifying what you like about yourself three times a day and write it in your superhero journal.

CHAPTER 5
THE SUPERHERO VALUES

Shadow awakes from yet another nightmare. They are getting less frequent but she still has them. This was one of the recurring ones. Lorion held her down and pushed himself on her. It hurt.

She trusted him. She also trusted herself to be able to keep herself safe but she never thought she'd have to protect herself from *him*. When he was finished, he left, leaving her to feel broken. Her once optimistic sense of the world for ever changed to believe that the world was a dangerous place, that she was unable to protect herself and, by extension, others.

And if that is the case, she thinks, *then what would be the point of doing this?*

By this, she means hunting demons. She sleeps with her crossbow under her pillow, always within her reach. Never feeling safe. Her Depression and Shame monsters have grown exponentially since then, taunting her about being 'weak', 'broken', and 'useless'.

The sexual assault she experienced clearly affected her in many areas of her life – social (she has withdrawn from the people in her life), emotional (developing PTSD and depression), professional (she stopped hunting), academic (her school grades suffered) and physical (by experiencing a lot of pain and tightness in her shoulders and pelvic area). Perhaps the biggest way that this traumatic experience affected her is by making it more challenging to engage in her core values.

Our core values are the most meaningful activities, life-paths and practices that we have. These might include being a great parent, being a supportive friend, being altruistic or heroic, being creative, healthy and many others. Engaging in our core values can be extremely beneficial for our physical and psychological health, while avoiding them can make us feel unfulfilled, putting us at a higher risk of depression and heart disease.

Sometimes our values might conflict with one another. For example, Doctor Semper values time travel, helping others, conducting scientific experiments and being a good friend. Occasionally when he is working on one of his scientific projects, he might not be able to spend as much time with his friends as he would like. This is completely normal and happens to most people. The trick is to observe which values we are able to engage in and which ones might need a bit more of our attention, and try to create a form of balance, while understanding that it may not always be possible.

Values are sometimes confused with goals, yet they are two different ideas. This is an important distinction to make because goals are finite, meaning that we can accomplish them and check them off our list. On the other hand, values are a lifelong direction, where the path of working on the specific values is itself the destination. A goal can also serve as a way to honour our values. For example, one of Neil's values is learning, which may be a lifelong journey. In order to work on this value, one of his goals is to graduate from the Wizarding College.

Unfortunately, our ability to participate in our values can at times be affected by difficult experiences, as in the cases of all our heroes in this book. For instance, Neil's biggest value is to be able to help others heal, physically or emotionally. In fact, he is hoping to become a healer after graduating. However, his social anxiety and his struggle with beliefs that he is 'not good enough' to be studying at the College, or that he is 'not important enough' to help anyone, prevent Neil from even attempting to reach out to others.

Yesterday, when Neil saw Shadow sitting by herself and crying, he felt his heart warm with compassion towards her. He envisioned himself coming up to her but ended up walking away from her, believing that he had nothing to contribute to make her feel better. Because he avoided engaging in his core values, Neil's Shame and Depression monsters began attacking him.

Do Neil and Shadow's struggles to honour their values sound familiar? Most likely, the answer is 'yes' because in fact, most of us have dealt with similar struggles. I find that one of the biggest struggles that holds people back from following their values is the mistaken belief that they do not matter, that they cannot make a difference. But what if you can?

The truth is that many of us do not even know how much we affect other people's lives. What if someone is alive today because of something kind you once said to them? What if there is someone out there who needs the very thing you have to offer? If anything were possible, what gift would you like to give to this world?

To think of it another way, I would like to ask these questions. Have you ever read a book or watched a movie and thought, *I wish I had those powers*? Whether it is super-strength, time-travelling abilities, teleportation or magical skills? What if you actually got them somehow? What if you were able to use your superpowers any way you wished, how would you use them? If there was a book or a movie about you to honour you after your death, what story would you want it to tell?

Hey, I know that you've been going through a hard time. I just wanted to say that I'm sorry about what happened to you and I'm here if you want to talk.

It's just so hard when the people who hurt you are the ones that were supposed to protect you.

I know. I'm so sorry. That's terrible. You don't have to go through it alone though.

Thanks. Neither do you.

See if you can write down an answer to these questions and identify some specific qualities that you might be able to work on in order to become that kind of superhero. Perhaps some of these values might be related to being courageous, heroic or compassionate. Perhaps they involve creativity, playfulness or inspiring others. By identifying and following these values, we might be able to start taking steps towards becoming the very kind of superhero that we want to be.

For example, Neil wants to be a knowledgeable wizard, someone who is a guide or a role model to others, someone who is able to help, inspire and heal others, and someone who would have the courage to ask Brian out on a date. His ideal life story is to be happily married one day, to be a supportive partner and a wonderful father. He wants to be a role model for equality and wants to be remembered as someone who made a difference.

Taking a courageous step in his valued direction, Neil approached Shadow and sat down next to her.

'Hey, I know that you've been going through a hard time. I just wanted to say that I'm sorry about what happened to you and I'm here if you want to talk,' he said to her.

He saw that Shadow's eyes were full of tears. 'It's just so hard when the people that hurt you are the ones that were supposed to protect you,' she replied.

'I know. I'm so sorry. That's terrible. You don't have to go through it alone though,' Neil said, feeling his anxiety leaving him.

'Thanks. Neither do you.'

IDENTIFYING YOUR CORE VALUES

An important part about identifying our values is knowing where we fall in terms of our efforts to honour them. The picture on the left shows a number of different clocks, all of which represent values that many people have. If you don't see one that is important to you, please feel free to write it in and if there are any that do not apply to you, feel free to disregard them.

The clocks do not have arrows, nor do they have any numbers on them. Instead, each of them has indicators to allow you to select whether the specific value is pursued 'too much', 'too little', 'not at all', or 'just right': Your task is to draw an arrow indicating where the specific value currently falls for you. For example, if you feel that you've been spending too much time working or studying, then your arrow will point toward, or closer to, 'too much'. On the other hand, if you feel that you have not been spending enough time and energy on your creative projects or your geeky interests, then your arrow would be pointing closer to 'too little.'

Remember that these values are yours and yours alone. These are meant to be your meaningful life directions, not ones dictated by society and other people in your life. This means that there might be certain values that you don't much care for and you are happy with the amount of time and effort you put into them. Then you can draw the arrow pointing toward 'just right' even if you don't much engage in them.

Take a look at the clocks altogether. What do you notice? If you are like me and the billions of other people out there, you might notice that many of your values are not where you would ideally like them to be. Some of your values might be completely neglected, while others are not met often enough and others might be overdone.

Learning where we are with our values and where we would like to be is one of the most important steps in superhero training, as it can allow us to figure out what being a superhero means to us. By reminding us which values we might need to focus on, we can start taking meaningful steps toward becoming a superhero and toward living our life more meaningfully and with fewer regrets.

SUPERHERO STEPS

Your assignment for this week is to practise identifying values, and work on picking one that you might be able to address. You might be able to, for example, text a friend in need to work on your 'friends' value or take a short walk to work on your 'health' value. This action does not need to be big and we will go into more detail about action steps in Chapter 9. In addition to working on your values, see if you can keep working on mindful gratitude – recognizing at least one thing you are grateful for every day and writing it down.

CHAPTER 6
THE DEFUSION CHARM

When Monica checked her phone this morning, there were no phone calls or texts from Lacey. It's been three days since they last spoke, and normally they speak every day.

Is she ignoring me? Monica thinks.

Monica tries calling her again. Voicemail.

Monica's Anxiety monster is only too happy to offer some worst-case scenarios. 'What if Lacey is mad at you? What if she hates you? Maybe she found out about all your cutting and binging stuff and now she doesn't want to be your friend any more. She's probably replaced you already.' Shame jumps in to offer her guidance: 'You're such a loser!'

When we feel anxious or insecure about something, our mind is likely to play out the worst-case scenario. Psychologists call this *catastrophizing*. The interesting thing about the worst-case scenarios is that most of them do not end up coming true. On any given day we might have several catastrophizing thoughts. For people with anxiety disorders, such as generalized anxiety disorder, for example, or obsessive-compulsive disorder, the frequency of their catastrophizing thoughts can sometimes be in the dozens or even hundreds per day. Now multiply this amount by 365 (the amount of days in a non-leap year) and then multiply the result by your age in years.

For example, if I approximate that I have on average ten catastrophizing thoughts per day, when I multiply that by 365, I get 3,650. When I then multiply that number by my age (thirty-two), I get 116,800. This is approximately how many catastrophizing thoughts I might have had in my lifetime. That is a lot! Now, how many of them actually came true? For me, to the best of my memory, that number is six.

What that means is that our mind is kind of like an unreliable psychic. Sure, she may be right once in a while, but mostly by chance alone. In fact, looking at the statistics above, it looks like the mind is only right 0.005per cent of the time.

That is less than 1 per cent, quite a bit less.

In fact, let's play this out. Suppose one of our heroes from this book, say Drovin, for example, went to a psychic who was as unreliable as the statistics I listed above. It might look something like this:

Psychic	–	'Your name begins with the letter M...'
Drovin (not amused)	–	'No.'
Psychic	–	'Letter J?'
Drovin	–	'No'
Psychic	–	'Letter D?'
Drovin	–	'Yes'
Psychic	–	'I KNEW it! You are going to be very rich, but be wary of anyone named Mike.'

Would you trust that psychic? Probably not, as he does not seem to be very good at what he does. And yet we blindly believe our mind when it does exactly the same thing. This is called *fusion*. This means that we are taking our thoughts as facts rather than mindfully noticing that they are just another thought, or another 'psychic' prediction our mind produced. For example, Neil believing that he is a 'fraud', that everyone at his university is smarter than he is, and that soon enough everyone is going to find out the truth about him, are all examples of cognitive fusion.

OUR MIND IS LIKE AN UNRELIABLE PSYCHIC

The problem with fusion is that when we start to believe some (often mistaken and unhelpful) thoughts that our minds produce, we are more likely to struggle with our monsters. In fact, fusion coupled with avoidance behaviours is a dangerous combination. For example, Doctor Semper fuses with the thought, 'If I walk too far away from the Simulator, I will be in danger.' Since in the given moment he fully believes that thought to be true, he is more likely to then avoid leaving the Simulator. As a result, he is stuck, completely controlled by his thoughts and his Anxiety monster.

The superhero tool that helps reduce fusion is called *defusion*. Defusion refers to reducing how much control a specific thought has over us. In the example above with Doctor Semper, it is clear that his mind has a lot of control over him and prevents him from following his values and living a meaningful life.

HOW DOES DEFUSION WORK?

I like to think of defusion as a kind of spell or a magic charm. And as is commonly done with regular magic charms, defusion often requires an incantation of sorts. There are a number of different ways to practise defusion charms and I want to give you a number of options, so that you can pick the one that works for you.

One such incantation requires that we repeat the distressing thought out loud for at least one to two minutes. This helps take the power and believability away from the thought and removes its meaning.

DEFUSION PRACTICE: THE DEFUSION REPETITION CHARM

For example, when Monica thinks, 'I'm fat,' she will probably feel overwhelmed with shame, she might feel sick to her stomach and disgusted with herself. She might also feel tense, sad, and angry with herself, and refuse to hang out with her friend, Lacey, for the fear that Lacey will notice how fat she is. This is an example of a fused thought, which prevents Monica from living a meaningful life. But what will happen if she tries the defusion charm, 'I'm fat, I'm fat, I'm fat…'? When she actually tries it, Monica notices that her thought no longer makes sense. In fact, she states that the words become meaningless. They no longer have the same power over her and she actually feels more power over them.

Give it a try.

What do you notice?

There are a number of different ways to use the defusion charm and the one we just learned is the *defusion repetition charm*. Another charm I like to use for battling against the dark magic of fusion is what I call the thought labelling defusion charm. The incantation for it goes like this: 'I'm having a thought that… [insert the thought you are having].' For example, Drovin fuses with the thought, 'I am a villain.' Because he takes this thought as fact, he avoids the people and activities that are meaningful to him. When I asked him to practise defusion, his defusion charm was, 'I'm having the thought that I'm evil.' When practicing this charm, Drovin noticed that there was a big difference in how he felt when he prefaced his fused thought with 'I'm having the thought that…' as opposed to when he did not. Mindfully recognizing that we are having a certain thought (or emotion) can often reduce its intensity and its hold over us.

Try it out. How did that go?

THE GRATITUDE DEFUSION CHARM

The next defusion charm is what I like to call *gratitude defusion*. This might sound strange but very often our mind is just trying to do its absolute best to protect us by imagining the worst possible scenarios. In some sense, it tries to predict every possible danger, however improbable it may be. It is kind of like an overprotective parent, one who worries too much about everything, including, but not limited to, space aliens kidnapping their child, dinosaurs taking over the world or zombies inhabiting the Earth. What would you say to such a parent? Probably something along the lines of, 'Thanks Mum/Dad, but I've got it from here.' That's exactly what we can also try to practise when it comes to our mind: 'Thanks, Mind, I'll be OK, I've got it from here.'

A person that especially liked this practice was Shadow. When working on this defusion charm, she realized that because she was highly affected by her trauma, her mind started imagining danger even when there wasn't any. In practising thanking her mind for trying to keep her safe, Shadow was able to see that her mind, while attempting to be helpful, was often unreasonable and overprotective.

Unlike many magic stunts you might see on television, defusion is one of those practices you can attempt at home. As with any magic, the effects of defusion may wear off. This means that you may need to continue using the charm repeatedly for full effect. There might be times when it is difficult, even if it was easy the day before. Give yourself a break, remind yourself of your values, and try again. You can do it, I believe in you.

SUPERHERO STEPS

Your superhero practise for this week includes practising defusion charms and practising gratitude on a daily basis.

WILLINGNESS TO FACE THE MONSTERS REDUCES THE
STRUGGLE AGAINST THEM

CHAPTER 7
THE ULTIMATE WEAPON –
THE SWORD OF WILLINGNESS

Katrina can still hear them. She lies down on her bed, trying to shield herself from her monsters. But they are relentless.

'What is wrong with you?' the Shame monster shouts at her.

The Anxiety monster chimes in: 'If you even attempt to drive, you will be in an accident again, especially if you drive alone or if you go past that intersection where it happened. It's NOT safe!'

The more Katrina tries to hide from them, the louder the monsters become. This tends to be the case for a lot of difficult emotional experiences. Trying to control our experiences is a losing battle. As we saw in Chapter 2, the more we try to control or avoid our thoughts or emotions, the more likely we are to experience them.

Here's a silly example. I would like you to imagine a pink unicorn, maybe one that looks a little bit like the one over the page. Can you visualize it? Can you see its pink body, its pink mane, and its pink horn?

Great!

Now what I'd like for you to do is close your eyes for one minute and do everything you can to NOT think of the pink unicorn. Don't imagine it. Don't think of the words 'pink' or 'unicorn' at all. Go!

TRY <u>NOT</u> TO THINK ABOUT THE PINK UNICORN

How did that go? Most people find this task to be nearly impossible to do. The very moment we are told not to think about something, that is usually all we think about. The same thing also applies to emotions. If someone offered you £1,000,000 not to like your favourite geek outlet, be it comic books, gaming, Cosplaying, TV shows or other values or favourite activities, could you do it? Could you actually force yourself to stop <u>liking</u> the things that are most meaningful to you?

The answer is 'no'. We cannot stop our feelings merely by ordering them to stop. We might be able to temporarily suppress them but what usually happens when we do that is that the blocked emotions end up coming out in other ways. For example, Katrina's attempts to control her driving anxiety might lead to her feeling anxious when she's in any other situation that she cannot control, such as being out with her friends.

However, what happens when Katrina stops running away from the monsters and looks at them for a while? They shrink! The more willing we are to engage our feared emotions, thoughts and other difficult internal experiences, the less intimidating they seem to become.

Katrina's initial attempts to control her driving anxiety were not successful but what was successful was her <u>willingness</u> to experience this discomfort in the service of her values. Willingness means agreeing to feel certain emotions that might make us uncomfortable, such as fear, sadness, anxiety and vulnerability. These emotions are not dangerous, though it sometimes might feel as if they are. We neither have to <u>like</u> experiencing these feelings, nor do we have to <u>want</u> them, we just need to be <u>willing</u> to experience them.

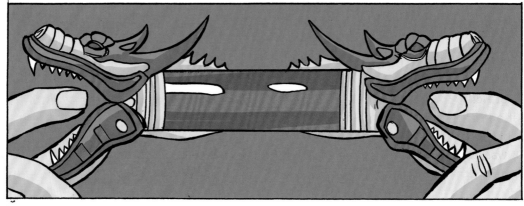

The willingness incorporates all emotions, including anger. Many people, like Drovin, might believe that anger is an unacceptable emotion as it can lead to aggression and violence. However, the emotion of anger and the act of aggression are two different things and while we may not be able to control how we feel, we can usually control what we do. In some instances, anger can even be protective, as it alerts us that we or someone we care about may be in danger and may need our protection. And just like the other emotions, the more we fight and try to suppress anger, the more we might experience it.

As an example of willingness, imagine that Neil picked up a Chinese finger trap at one of his classes at the Wizarding College. Curious, but not knowing what it was, Neil analysed the strange device until his own fingers got caught in it. Naturally being quite anxious and also worrying about getting into trouble with the teacher, Neil attempted to remove the strange device from his fingers but noticed that the more he tried to pull his fingers out, the tighter the trap became. After many of his other attempts to set himself free failed miserably, Neil did what he thought was unthinkable: he pushed his fingers deeper into the trap. To his surprise and deep relief, the trap came loose and Neil was able to free his fingers.

Our emotions are kind of like the finger trap. The more we try to avoid or control them, the stronger they might become over time. However, the more open we are to experiencing them, the less likely we are to struggle with them over time. Think of it as like having coffee/tea with your monsters and getting to know them a little bit. Many people, like Monica for example, find out that when they get to know their monsters, the monsters seem to have less of an impact on them.

WHAT WILLINGNESS IS AND ISN'T

Willingness is not:

- Tolerating abuse
- Accepting injustice
- Giving in or giving up
- Pushing beyond your limit

Willingness is:

- Agreeing to experience any internal emotions that might show up on your superhero journey. These might include anxiety, insecurity, depression and fusion with thoughts, such as 'I can't do it.'
- Being vulnerable enough to say 'I love you' first, to take a chance on something that is extremely important to you because opportunities like that don't always present themselves. Being vulnerable has been shown to be beneficial for people's well-being and for improving their relationships.
- Being courageous. Some people believe that 'courage' means not having any fear. That is not accurate. Courage actually means doing what you believe in despite being afraid or struggling with physical or emotional pain.

If it feels scary to open up to feeling your emotions, you are not alone. It's scary for everyone. And at the same time, that is exactly the kind of superhero skill that makes us wholesome, heroic, and willing to take a chance on life.

When I first started working on this book, all kinds of insecurities ran through my mind. Things like, 'What if I can't write it?' 'What if it comes out terribly?'

That was my Anxiety monster talking. Then the Shame monster showed up with 'You're an amateur! You've never written a book before. You have no idea what you're talking about!' The Anger monster caused me to get angry at myself and want to rip up the pages. The Depression monster then came in to add the final punch: 'This is hopeless. Just give up.'

And you know what? I did. After receiving numerous heart-wrenching rejections from publishers and agents, I did give up. I believed the monsters, I fused with the thoughts they created and I tried to control my feelings by shutting down and not trying. After a few months of this I was miserable. My monsters were louder than ever and I felt as though my life didn't have a purpose. Finally, I realized that I needed to go through my values list and what I saw made me very sad. I saw that I was not engaging at all in the most important values to me: creativity, compassion and supporting others through my writing.

I decided to practise what I preached to my patients – willingness. I was willing to open up to more potential heartbreak and failure. Somehow through it all I found my courage and was later found by and signed with a publisher that my 'amateur' insecure self-identity would have never even allowed me to apply to work with. I'm over the moon about being able to work on this book and what this experience has taught me is that when we are willing to take chances, we are more likely to get what we really want than when we don't even try.

It might be hard to do that when the monsters are especially rambunctious, but in a way, that's what they do. The monsters' role, at least in some ways, is to keep us safe – safe from embarrassing ourselves, safe from danger, safe from being overwhelmed, however wrong they might be. If we openly engage with them, we just might be able to befriend them after all.

SUPERHERO STEPS

This week your task is opening up to your thoughts and feelings that you're willing to experience for something that's very important to you, such as a core value or something on your 'bucket list.' In addition, continue to practise gratitude daily.

81

Raise your hand if you are ever hard on yourself, if you call yourself bad names or put yourself down.

CHAPTER 8
SETTING UP YOUR SECRET LAIR WITH SELF-COMPASSION

'**C**'mon, you coward! Stop being so whiny and go out there!' Doctor Semper's Shame monster is nearly hoarse yelling at him today.

A strange thing happens when we struggle with a physical or mental difficulty. Rather than being kind and compassionate to ourselves, we tend to attack ourselves when we are feeling bad. We kick ourselves while we are down and, rather than addressing the situation, only shame ourselves for feeling bad. Kristin Neff, a famous self-compassion researcher, says that when we are being hard on ourselves, 'we are both the attacker and the attacked.'

On the one hand, it might seem that by criticizing ourselves we are getting more motivated to get going. In fact, that's what a lot of people believe. But is that really the case?

Doctor Semper sits on the floor of the Simulator. His chest feels tight and empty at the same time. He feels a lump in his throat as he is fighting back tears. His Depression monster is already telling him about how hopeless his situation is and how he will never get better.

Criticizing ourselves at a time of crisis makes a setback so aversive that we might not be willing to try again. Think about it. If every time you didn't succeed in something, your friends or parents shamed you for it, making you feel guilty and worthless on top of already feeling devastated about the loss, how would that feel? Sadly, I know that for many of you this might not be an unfamiliar feeling. So often we get put down when we need support and encouragement.

Whether or not you had the level of support that you needed during some of the most difficult times of your life, we can try a new skill, a skill of self-compassion. Self-compassion refers to providing ourselves with kindness and support when we are going through a hard time. In fact, I believe that most of us are far more supportive of the people we care about than of ourselves. Think about it, when your friend has a bad day, how do you treat them? And how do you treat yourself?

Most people tend to be very supportive when a friend or a family member is struggling, perhaps offering a hug, encouragement or a shoulder to lean on. However, when we ourselves are struggling, we tend to yell at ourselves, feeling ashamed for feeling bad. But what if we treated ourselves with the same level of compassion as we treat our favourite people (or pets)?

It might look something like this: we might notice that painful emotion, thought or physical sensation in the body. We might offer ourselves some words of encouragement, such as, 'It's OK, darling. I know this is scary. Many people get anxious sometimes.' We might even offer ourselves a little hug by placing the palms of our hands on our heart in order to further support ourselves. Or perhaps we would notice that we need some social support or a little break and perhaps be able to honour these needs. How would that feel?

Over the years of me talking about self-compassion with my patients and students, I've experienced mixed reactions. Some people love the idea of self-compassion and are excited to try it. At the same time others are apprehensive, stating that it feels 'fake' or 'too fluffy.' There are also people that get very sad as they realize that they have never been compassionate to themselves before, while others believe that self-compassion is 'selfish.'

Whichever category you fall into (including a completely separate one) you are not alone. Some people are excited about self-compassion while others are hesitant to try it. However, most people who practice self-compassion report feeling better.

ELEMENTS OF SELF-COMPASSION

Self-compassion consists of three elements: mindfulness, common humanity, and self-kindness. You have already learned about the superhero skill of mindfulness in Chapter 3. In this case, *mindfulness* refers to the ability to notice when we are going through a hard time, when we might feel sad or anxious, or experience physical pain. Most of us when we experience some kind of a painful physical or psychological difficulty, might try to avoid it or push through it. Unfortunately, as we saw in Chapter 2, avoidance does not work very well and in fact can make us feel worse in the long term.

Instead of avoiding the painful experience, self-compassion teaches us to offer kindness to ourselves. Self-kindness could mean offering ourselves a hug, hugging a pillow, a pet or a stuffed animal, breathing, meditating, taking a break, drinking tea, or another self-care practice.

In addition, self-compassion teaches us about common humanity, which refers to the idea that we are not alone in our painful experience. In fact, many other people also struggle with something like this, meaning that this is a very human and a very real experience. These practices are meant to allow us to feel less alone in our struggles while also offering ourselves the support that we might really need at that time.

Some of the common obstacles to self-compassion include:

- The belief that self-compassion practice might make us lazier, more indulgent and less likely to continue pushing ourselves to succeed
- The belief that self-compassion is 'weak' or 'selfish'
- The idea that self-compassion takes a long time to practise and that people do not have time for it

Interestingly, while these obstacles tend to be among the most commonly used reasons for why people do not practise or struggle with practicing self-compassion, the actual research points to the opposite of these being true. Specifically, the research suggests that people who practise self-compassion are likely to be more resilient to a setback and are therefore less likely to give up. In addition, these people seem to have an easier time being compassionate and supportive to others.

If you have ever flown on an aeroplane, you might remember the flight attendants' message that if the cabin pressure should drop, oxygen masks will be available for passengers. The passengers are instructed to secure their own mask before assisting others. This is because if we are unconscious, we are unable to help others. When we practise self-compassion, we are in essence building resilience against many potential stressors and challenges that we might face, potentially allowing us to be more helpful to others. Think of it like a healing potion in a video game, one that replenishes your health back to full potential.

Finally, self-compassion does not have to be time consuming. Of course, extended vacations can be replenishing but if time is limited, we can practise *self-compassion on the go*. This includes brief self-care practices, such as:

- Placing your hands on your heart   • Breathing exercises
- Hugging a pillow   • Cuddling with your pet
- Taking a one-minute (or even a thirty- second) stretch or walk break
- Performing an activity you like (such as singing) while doing an activity you have to do (such as driving or showering)
- Talking kindly to yourself, such as 'I know this is hard, sweetheart. I'm so sorry. I'm here with you.'

If, however, you find that you have a few extra minutes, a very helpful self-compassion practice involves writing letters to yourself. In this exercise, you would first write a letter to yourself from the point of view of a self-critic, listing all the mean, nasty things that you might say to yourself. Then write another letter to yourself as if you were writing to a dear friend who is speaking to him- or herself in that way. Notice how each of these exercises feels and how you feel after you have completed it.

Some people report feeling a mixture of sweetness and sorrow when they complete the letter-writing exercise, while others might feel deep emotional pain. Any of these reactions are normal, and sometimes when we open up an old wound it might initially hurt, until we allow it to heal properly. When we first begin to explore an extremely painful topic, we might sometimes be overwhelmed with emotion. This is called *backdraft*. At the time when it hurts so much to open up to a specific emotion, we can also offer ourselves some self-compassion through a personal hug and a gentle message. It is also not necessary to push ourselves beyond our limits. We can open our heart to the extent that we are able and then close it again, and continue to practise opening it as time passes. This is a softer, gentler approach to facing our traumatic losses and other painful experiences, one at a time.

For Shadow, her anger at herself for not being able to protect herself from Lorion caused her to develop self-hatred. Both Drovin and Doctor Semper experienced the same thing about their inability to protect the people they cared about. However, in practising self-compassion, they were, in a way, able to comfort and soothe their own monsters and begin an internal healing process. In fact, practising self-compassion and compassion toward others has been shown through research to be extremely beneficial to our health. Specifically, practicing compassion allows our body to release a special kind of hormone, oxytocin, also known as the 'love hormone,' or the 'cuddle hormone'. This hormone is often released when we are hugging someone or when we see an adorable little kitten, puppy or other cute things. This hormone makes us feel safe and supported and has positive effects on our heart and immune system. In addition, compassion practices have been shown through research to reduce PTSD, depression, anxiety and chronic pain symptoms, and make it easier for people to reduce cravings, including drug and food cravings, as well as make it easier to socialize with others.

In a way, practising self-compassion is kind of like being in our own safe space, in our own superhero lair, except that you can take it with you anywhere. Creating a safe environment for yourself can allow you to find the strength and courage that you might need in order to grow as a superhero.

Therefore, this week we are going to practise the most courageous step yet: self-compassion.

SUPERHERO STEPS

Practise embracing your monsters by supporting yourself when difficult emotions show up – embracing yourself (hands on heart), hugging a pillow, breathing, or another exercise. In addition, see if you can practise writing a self-compassionate letter to yourself. Finally, practise doing something nice for yourself without having to earn it and, as always, practice mindful gratitude daily.

CHAPTER 9
TAKING SUPERHERO ACTION STEPS

Monica rereads the text message for the sixth time: 'Lacey attempted to commit suicide. She slashed her wrists. She's at the hospital.'

Her fingers trembling, her heart pounding, Monica is finally able to dial Lacey's father's phone to find out which hospital Lacey is in and rush over there.

Often our assumptions and fused thoughts might make us assume that we are alone in our experiences and that the reason why someone might ignore us has something to do with our own inadequacies. Monica thought Lacey ignoring her texts meant that Lacey was mad at her or hated her. In fact, Lacey, like Monica, was also struggling with her own Depression and Shame monsters.

When Monica arrives at the hospital, Lacey is extremely embarrassed to tell her that she'd been struggling with depression, cutting and suicidal thoughts for several years. Seeing her best friend hurting so much both hurts and warms Monica's compassionate heart. She sits with Lacey, holds her hand and then shows her friend the scars from her own hand. Her own heart is beating very fast and her Anxiety monster is terrified of being so open about her own struggle, but both girls hug and cry together, feeling more connected and less misunderstood.

Lacey's suicide attempt made Monica realize that she was not the only one struggling with depression. She was anxious and afraid but her newly found sense of purpose – connecting with her values of helping others – gave her the courage she never knew she had. Monica asked her school's permission to make an announcement during the student assembly. Her hands shaking and her heart pounding, she approached the podium. When she looked down at the audience, Lacey looked up at her with a smile, her hands still in bandages.

Monica knew that she wanted to begin spreading awareness about the effects of depression and eating disorders on people's lives. Her voice was shaking when she began her speech.*

'I wanted to share my story with all of you. I struggle with depression. I also have bulimia and when things get really tough, I cut. I've gotten some help recently and I'm starting to feel better although it's still challenging at times. I wanted to let all of you know in case any of you struggle with these or other mental health or physical conditions. You don't have to go through it alone.'

When Monica was finished, she had tears running down her face. She was not the only one crying, however. Students and teachers alike were crying too. Lacey was crying and smiling at the same time. The entire school stood up to applaud Monica's courageous and encouraging speech. Afterwards, many students opened up to her about their own struggles with depression and other disorders.

Monica is an example of an inspiring hero who, despite her monsters' shouting, was able to courageously reach out and help hundreds of other students who were struggling with mental health difficulties. Being a hero therefore means taking mindful steps that are in line with our values that we identified in Chapter 5. It means that even though we might still struggle with our monsters, we can practise all or some of the previously learned skills, like defusion, mindfulness, self-compassion, willingness and connecting with our superhero self in order to actively take superhero actions toward our values.

* This account is based on a true story of one of my incredibly courageous patients, who opened up to her schoolmates about her struggles and helped many other students see that they were not alone.

We can try this by first connecting with our own heroes. Is there a hero you really identify with, real or fictional? Perhaps someone you look up to, someone you wish you could be more like? Now see if you can think of or try to imagine what this person's values might be – courage, heroism, creativity or something else? What might have been some of the obstacles they have faced and how might they have worked on them?

One of my biggest real life heroes is a famous fantasy novelist, Neil Gaiman. He is incredibly talented as a writer and extremely supportive of and encouraging to his fans. I always just assumed that he was quite confident and had no obstacles to overcome in his career. Of course, looking back at it, this thought is clearly a silly one, as everyone struggles at least at some point, even the most successful people. I once saw Mr Gaiman do an interview for one of his novels. When asked if he ever feels insecure, he said that not only does he sometime feel insecure, but that there have been many times when he felt like a fraud and the 'Fraud Police' would find out. This interview made me see things in a very different light. It really highlighted an aspect of common humanity for me – that everyone struggles with insecurity but not everyone talks about it. Hearing my hero talk about his own struggle inspired me to talk and write about mine. What is interesting about that is that the more I talked about it, the more courageous I felt, allowing me to more closely follow my own values – courage, authenticity, compassion, creativity and helping others.

Let's take a few moments to write down the answers to these questions in your superhero journal in order to help you begin taking leaps in your superhero career. What do you value? What are the obstacles? Which skills might be helpful in dealing with at least some of these obstacles?

One of the biggest obstacles that holds many people back from being their full superhero self is an *attachment to outcome*. Attachment to outcome means having a specific and rigid idea of a goal. For example, becoming a best-selling author/artist, being selected for a job promotion, or being graciously thanked for a good deed. Of course, it would be nice to get what we want. However, sometimes when we are holding on to those desires too rigidly, we are essentially setting ourselves up for disappointment. If things do not go our way or if our goal is not met then we might feel devastated. Rather than becoming overly attached to a specific outcome, we can practise taking non-attached steps (where possible) toward our valued direction. This might mean continuing to work on your creativity, career, or relationship because it is important to you rather than because you expect a certain kind of reward. Practising more flexibility in our values can allow us the freedom to explore what is truly important to us and potentially allow us to grow and develop in that area, often making us feel more fulfilled than when we have a set expectation of an outcome.

For example, when Doctor Semper first began traveling around the universe in his Simulator, he expected that he should always be able to save everyone he met. While that is an admirable goal, it is an unrealistic one and when he was unable to save a little girl, he was naturally devastated. The truth is that just about anyone in his situation would be heartbroken if they failed to save someone. However, Doctor Semper experienced the kind of guilt and trauma that many doctors, firefighters, police officers, paramedics and other first responders and crisis workers often experience. The loss itself was of course excruciating. However, the attachment to the outcome added to his traumatic experience, making it difficult for him to recover, and triggering his panic attacks and agoraphobia.

In working toward his values of trying to help people, Doctor Semper drops off Drovin back on his home planet of Kridaq. Drovin is hesitant to go inside and Semper graciously offers to walk with him. As the two begin to approach Drovin's old family home, Doctor Semper notices that his hearts have started pounding in his chest and he begins to sweat. His Anxiety monster is shouting at him to stop but the Doctor compassionately reassures his monster and continues to walk with his friend.

When the men enter, Drovin's son runs up to him, excited to see him, and his wife is in tears, happy to see him as well. In taking the most challenging step for him – self-compassion – Drovin is able to begin to practise self-forgiveness and is able to connect with his biggest value – his family. And for the first time in a long time he knows what he is grateful for.

DAD!

This. I'm grateful for this.

Katrina is also facing her fears as she drives to join Shadow and Neil at the Wizarding College after the trio find out about the College being taken over by demons. Katrina is terrified. Her palms are sweating, her shoulders are tense, there are times when she holds her breath, her heart is beating loudly in her chest and her Anxiety monster is insisting that she is unsafe. Normally, Katrina would have listened to her monster and avoided driving; however, this time she has a mission – to help her friends stop the demons' attack. She buckles herself and her monster in and starts the ignition. The car starts moving. Katrina's anxiety initially spikes so much that her vision gets blurry, but after a few moments the blurriness begins to dissipate. Sometimes spiking up and sometimes reducing to more manageable levels, Katrina's anxiety stays with her but so does her courage.

When they get to Wizarding College, Neil and Shadow quickly run to try to help out the remaining teachers and students who are being threatened by demons. Neil sees that Brian is among those who are captured. His anxiety increases but so does his anger and his adrenaline.

Usually these physiological sensations – the shallow breathing, sweating, the tension in his shoulders – make Neil very uncomfortable but today he has a purpose: to use his expertise and magic to save others. After using his own defusion charm and self-compassion magic potions, Neil feels stronger and more prepared. He then shoots a fireball toward the demons that are holding the hostages. He is able to release the hostages in a single spell but the demons are relentless. Two of them grab his arms and attempt to capture him.

When Shadow sees her friend in danger she feels a surge of anger running through her body.

Shadow has not felt this courageous and invigorated in months. Her hunter instincts kick in and she grabs the demons one by one and pulls them off Neil. She then single-handedly defeats more than two dozen demons, helping Neil and his classmates save the school from a certain invasion. Feeling invigorated and reunited with her life purpose, Shadow turns to check on Neil and sees him walking away with Brian. The two wizards are holding hands. She smiles. She feels different... content.

These are just the beginnings of the journeys taken by our heroes, who continue to work on taking steps in their valued directions. That is not to say that they never struggle, because they do, often. However, the new connection with their valued direction gave them the courage and the motivation to continue on their superhero, journey and the skills they learned helped them reduce their struggles with their own monsters.

And now it is your turn to become a superhero. You might not believe it but you are ready now. Put on your cape/cloak/trench coat and let's begin. Today is the day you can take your first step (or perhaps not even the first) to being a real superhero. You might want to write down today's date, because today is when it all begins. Taking a look at your values, which one can you work on today? Which skills would be helpful to you in this process?

SUPERHERO STEPS

Challenge yourself to take a step in one of your valued directions every day. These do not have to be major life-changing directions. Start small and keep working from there. Record your progress every day and continue working on mindful gratitude. Here is a recommended gratitude practice for this week: write a letter to someone you are grateful to and, if possible, send it to that person. If that individual is no longer living or is a fictional character, then write the letter and read it out loud to yourself.

CHAPTER 10
LEVELLING UP IN LIFE

Congratulations! You have completed your training at the Superhero Training Academy. I'm incredibly proud of you and all your hard work. It takes a lot of courage to face our own fears and follow our own valued paths. I therefore now pronounce you a superhero.

As you probably know, superheroing takes a lot of hard work and is a never-ending process. Rather, it is a life-long practice. Let's spend some time talking about how you can continue superheroing and levelling up in real life.

First, let us take a look at your values again and see if anything has changed. Over the page you once again will see a picture of the clocks displaying the different values that you might have. Draw in an arrow for each one indicating if you are putting in 'too much', 'too little', 'not at all', or 'just the right' amount of time into each of these values. What did you notice? How do they compare to those in Chapter 5? Did anything change? What still needs to be worked on?

It is perfectly normal for some values to shift while others might remain the same, or even get worse. Superhero work is a constant adjustment of our steps in order to balance and honour all the meaningful values we have.

IDENTIFYING YOUR CORE VALUES

106

Let us review some of the takeaway messages from what you might have learned. First and most important – avoidance almost always feels better in the short term and almost always leads to worsening symptoms in the long term. Therefore, there is actually a high cost to avoidance – not living your life and allowing the villains to win. Instead, we can utilize some of the skills you learned in this book (and possibly from other sources as well) in order to help you take more superhero steps in your valued direction.

Some of these skills include:
- The willingness to experience difficult emotions, thoughts, and physical sensations
- Conjuring a defusion charm in order to reduce the believability of our thoughts
- Using mindfulness to observe your experiences
- Staying true to your superhero self, no matter the situation or environment you are in
- Practicing self-compassion (the healing potion), which allows you to be kind to yourself and to realize that you are not alone in your struggle
- Identifying your values and taking steps to meet them

In fact, I would imagine that you have already begun the process of change and we can take a look at the same survey you initially filled out to assess whether anything has changed.

1. My symptoms overwhelm me — T/F
2. I must get rid of my depression/anxiety/shame/anger — T/F
3. I spend most of my time worrying about the future — T/F
4. I spend a lot of my time fixating on the past — T/F
5. My self-critical thoughts (such as 'I'm not good enough' or 'I'm not attractive enough') have become my identity — T/F
6. I don't spend enough time doing things I care about — T/F
7. I am unhappy with many aspects of my life — T/F

What did you notice? Did anything change? What still needs to be worked on?

Keep in mind that it is perfectly normal to continue to struggle in some areas. In fact, Monica and Neil still struggle with some of their monsters at times, and Katrina does too, but overall they are getting better. It is also normal to have setbacks, especially after a drastic life change but most people find that once they are able to get back to practising their skills again, they are able to get back into the rhythm faster than they did when they initially began the training.

PROBLEM-SOLVING SETBACKS - ARE YOU EXPECTING TOO MUCH TOO SOON?

One of the biggest reasons for setbacks has to do with our expectations for quick results. Every major project takes a lot of time and effort, and progress does not always go in a linear fashion. This means that some days we might do better than others and some days we might struggle with something that was not an issue before. This is where willingness and self-compassion skills are especially important. The more willing we are to experience a setback and the more we can be kind to ourselves, the more likely we are to succeed.

For example, have you ever tried to diet? Have you ever told yourself, starting Monday I'm never eating unhealthy sugary foods again and I am going to exercise every day? If you have, then chances are that such a rigid plan most likely was not successful. Unfortunately, what often happens when we do not succeed is that we become really hard on ourselves and give up trying altogether.

In one research study looking at the effects of criticism rigidity vs. self-compassion on healthy eating behaviours, participants, who were on a diet, were asked to eat a doughnut. Half of them were later taught a self-compassion practice – to be kind to themselves as everyone indulges once in a while. The other half of the research participants were not taught to practise self-compassion. All the participants were later asked to participate in a 'taste-test' where they would be able to eat as many candy pieces as they wished in order to rate them on the different taste properties. What did the researchers find? The participants who were not taught self-compassion ate twice as much candy as the ones who were taught self-compassion. This suggests that when we are able to forgive ourselves for experiencing setbacks, which are inevitable, we are more likely to be able to continue on our heroic journey.

INTENTION SETTING AND PRACTICE

One of the best ways to continue on your superhero quest is to practise daily intention setting. Specifically it means setting one or two small, achievable goals for that day that would be in line with your values. At the end of the day, be sure to celebrate your successes and re-evaluate your setbacks.

This is very important: the process of daily evaluations of your successes and setbacks is by no means intended to create self-criticism for what you were unable to achieve. It is painful enough to have a setback, and as we saw from the above-mentioned research, criticism and giving into our Shame monster can actually set us back even more. Instead, look at it as an opportunity, a heroic challenge. If every hero accomplished everything he or she wanted with ease and without any struggle, their stories would be boring and we would not enjoy them. Instead, we often see our favourite heroes try a quest sometimes unable to initially succeed, but often able to continue and eventually succeed. This is a similar practice. And in this practice it is as important, if not more important, to celebrate your successes as to note your setbacks.

And with this message, I leave you, my hero. Keep superheroing, you can save the world. I'm proud of you.

SUPERHERO STEPS

Here is your last assigned practice. Set aside some time weekly or every few weeks to reread one of the chapters and practice that skill. You can go in order or based on the current need.

KEEP SUPERHEROING!

THE
IMPR⟳VEMENT
ZONE

Looking for life inspiration?

The Improvement Zone has it all, from **expert advice** on how to advance your **career**, improve your **relationships**, boost your **business**, revitalise your **health** or develop your **mind**. Whatever your goals, head to our website now.

www.improvementzone.co.uk

INSPIRATION ON THE MOVE

INSPIRATION DIRECT TO YOUR INBOX